A COURSE

OF

COUNTERPOINT

AND

FUGUE,

BY

L. CHERUBINI,

MEMBER OF THE FRENCH INSTITUTE,
DIRECTOR OF THE CONSERVATORIO OF MUSIC IN PARIS,
OFFICER OF THE LEGION OF HONOUR, ETC.

TRANSLATED BY

J. A. HAMILTON.

AUTHOR OF THE MUSICAL CATECHISMS, GRAMMAR, DICTIONARY, ETC. ETC.

SECOND EDITION.

This Work is adopted as the Code of Instruction in Composition for the Classes of the French Conservatory.

VOL. II.

LONDON:

PUBLISHED BY R. COCKS AND CO

20, PRINCES STREET, HANOVER SQUARE:

Musicsellers in ordinary to Her Majesty Queen Victoria.

SOLD ALSO BY MESSRS. SIMPKIN, MARSHALL, AND CO. STATIONERS' COURT.

MDCCCXLI.

WINDHAM PRESS
CLASSIC REPRINTS

STRICT FUGUE

in TWO PARTS.

Engraved by M. Trenklee.

Episode composed of fragments of the Subject.
Subject in the relative Minor mode.
Answer curtailed.
Episode.

Subject in the
Minor of the Supertonic & curtailed.
Episode.

Modulation to the Minor of the original Key.
Stretto.
Answer.
Subject.
Subject.
Answer.

Episode.
Dominant Pedal in
Subject.
the upper part.
Answer.
Dominant Pedal in the lower part.

TONAL FUGUE

in TWO PARTS.

Counter-subject.
Answer.
Subject.
Counter-subject.
Episode composed of a fragment of the Counter-subj.
Subject in the sub-dominant.
Answer.
Counter-subj.

Episode compd. of a fragment of the Subj. in imitation.
Subject in the relative Minor.
Counter-subj.
Counter-subj.
Answer.
Codetta.
Counter-subj.
Subject.

Subject in the supertonic.
Fragment of the Subject in imitation.
Counter-subj.
Fragment of the Counter-subj. in imitation.
Another fragment of the Subj. imitated in the 2nd
Idem.
Fragment of the Counter subj. imitated in the 4th

Subject.
Stretto.
Answer closer to
the Subject.
Fragment of the Counter-subj. in imitation.
Answer.
Subject.
Fragment of the Counter-subj. in imitat.n
Episode.

Subject.
Answer still closer.
Episode.
Subject.
Episode.
Subject in answer to the subj.

Subject.
Answer.
Episode.
Subject inverted.
Close answer to the subj. inverted.

STRICT FUGUE in THREE PARTS.

This Fugue by the nature of its Subject, requires a frequent use of the chromatic genus; and from its melodial figures and the multiplicity of notes, it possesses somewhat of an instrumental character.

Answer.
2d. Counter-subject.
1st. Counter subject.
Imitation.
Episode comp^d. of a fragment of the 1st. Counter-subject.
Imitation.
2d. Counter-subj.
Answer.
Codetta.

2d. Counter-subject.
Subject.
Episode composed of divers imitations of
1st. Counter-subject.
the subject & 1st. Counter-subject.

Subject inverted.
1st Counter-subject inverted.
Answer to inverted Subj.
1st Counter-subject inverted.
Counter-subj. inverted.
Subject inverted.

Answer.
Counter-subj. inverted.
Episode.
Counter-subject to the new subject.
New subject composed of the End of the Codetta to 1st subject.
Answer to the new subject.
Counter-subject.

New Subject.
New Counter-subject.
Counter-subj.
Episode.
Answer.

Stretto.
1st Subject.
1st Coun-
ter-subject.
Answer closer
to subject.

Answer.
Counter-subject.
Subject.
Episode.
Answer.
Subject still nearer.

Subject.
Imitation.
Episode.

Answer.
Stretto on a Pedal.
Subj.
Pedal.
2d Counter-subj.
Episode.
Imitation.

Fragment of the Counter-subject to new subject in imitation.

TONAL FUGUE in THREE PARTS, with ONE COUNTER SUBJECT.

Part ad libitum.
Subj.
Counter-subj.
Answer.
Codetta.
Counter-subj.
Part ad libitum.
Episode composed of a part of the Counter-subj. in imitation.

Modulation into the
sub-dominant.
The same to the relative Minor Key.
Return to the principal Key.
Imitation of
Counter-subj. curtailed with modulation.
Subject curtailed.
Imitation of the Counter-subj.
the subject in the 9th. or 2d.
Imitation in the 3rd.
Episode.
Counter-subj. curtailed.

Subject in
the sub-dominant curtailed.
Counter-subject curtailed.

Counter-subject imitated.
Subject in the relative Minor curtailed in imitation of the subject in
the sub-dominant.
Second imitation in the Minor mode of the mediant.
Counter-subj.
Episode.

Stretto.
Subject.
Answer.
Subject.
Answer.
Answer.
Subject.

Episode.
Answer.
Subject.
Pedal.

Subject.
Answer.

TONAL FUGUE in FOUR PARTS,

with ONE COUNTER SUBJECT.

Codetta comp.[d] of a new melodial passage as a theme for the Episode.

Counter-subj.
added part.
Answer.
new melodial figure.
Episode.

Answer.
Counter-subject.
added part.
Counter-subj.
Subject.

Episode.

Subject in the relative Major.
Counter-subject.
Subject in the sub-dominant serving as an answer.
Counter-subject.

Episode.
Fragment of the subj. serving as a motive for this Episode.
Imitation.
Imitation.
Imitation.

New figure.
New figure.

Stretto.
Counter-subject.
Answer.
Subject.
Episode.
Counter-subject.

Subject.
Imitation.
Counter-subject.
Subj.
Answer.

Counter-subj.
Answer.
Counter-subj.
Subject by augmentation.
Answer by augmentn.

Subject.
Answer.
Subject.
Pedal.
Answer.
New melodial figure.

TONAL FUGUE in FOUR PARTS,

and with TWO COUNTER SUBJECTS.

2d C.S.
1st C.S.
Subject.
added part.
1st C.S.
Answer.
2d C.S.

Episode.
Imitation.
Fragment of 2d C.S.
Fragment of 1st C.S.
Answer.
added part.
1st C.S.

2d C.S.
2d C.S.
added part.
1st C.S.
Subject.
1st C.S.
added part.
Answer.

2d C.S.
Subject.
2d C.S.
1st C.S.
Episode.
Imitation of a fragment of the added part.

Fragment of
the 1st C.S.
Imitation.

2d C.S.
Fragment of the Subject.

1st C.S.
2d C.S.
Subject in the sub-dominant.
Answer to the Subject in the sub-dominant.
1st C.S.
2d C.S.

added part.
Subject in the relative Minor.
2d C.S.
1st C.S.
1st C.S.
added part.
Answer.

2d C.S.
Episode.

Stretto.
Subject.
Answer.

Subject.
Answer.

Answer.
Subject.
Answer.
Subject.
Counter-subj: closer.

1st C.S.
Answer.
Pedal.
Answer.
Subject.
2d C.S.
1st C.S.
Subject.
Answer.
Subject.

Chromatic Fugue in Four Parts With Three Counter Subjects.

The Subject of this Fugue belongs to a Tonal Fugue, since it at first decends from the Tonic to the Dominant; the Answer therefore ought to proceed from the Dominant to the Tonic.

Example of the Answer. according to the Rules of the Tonal-Fugue.

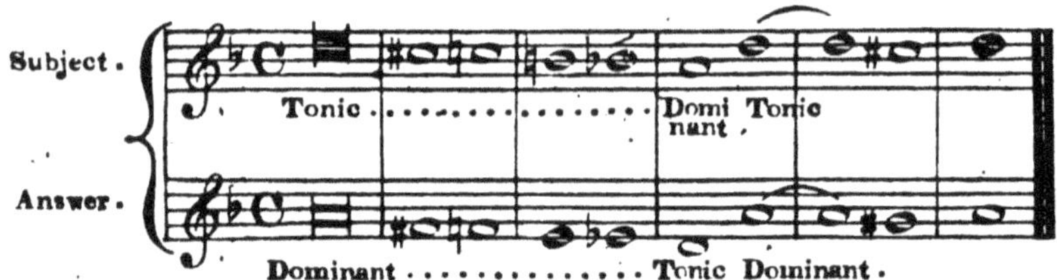

But this Answer would have rendered the treatment of the Counter Subjects very difficult, and would have required frequent alterations; we have therefore considered it better to treat it as a strict Fugue.

This Fugue from the manner in which it is conducted, and by the very nature of the Subject, may be regarded as a *Fugue of Intonation*.

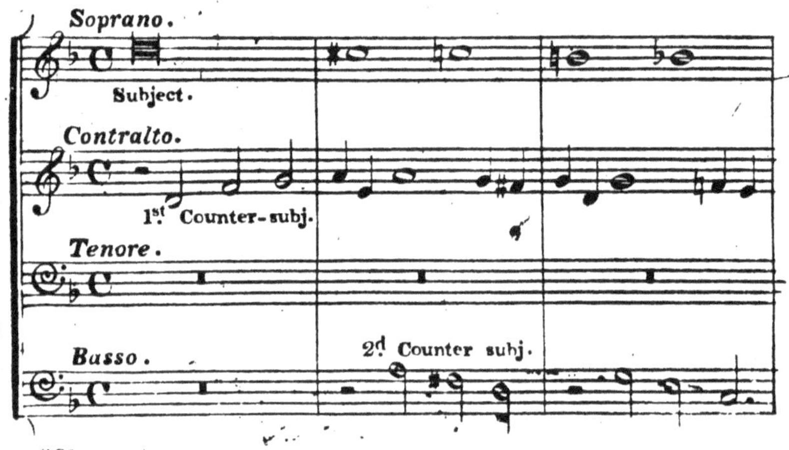

Codetta leading to
3d Counter subj.
the Answer.
Answer.
2d C.S.
1st Counter-subj.
3d C.S.

Codetta leading to the reply of the Subject.
added part or ad libitum
imitating the 2d Counter-subj.
2d C.S.
Subject.
1st C.S.
3rd C.S.
Codetta.

1st C.S.
added part.
2d C.S.
Answer.
3rd C.S.
Fragment of the subj.
by diminution.
Episode.

Fragment of the 3d C.S.
Answer.
1st C.S.
added part.
2d C.S.

Imitation of this
New Counter-subject to this fragment of the subj.
Subject curtailed, entering before the end of the Answer
and serving as a motive for the Episode.
Imitation of the new Counter-subject.
fragment of the subject.
Fragment of the 3d Counter-subject.
Fragment of the 2d Counter-subject.

Subject introduced in this Episode; but with only one of the old Counter-subjects, and the new Counter-subject.
1st C.S.
New Counter-subj.
Part ad libitum.
3d Counter-subj.
Continuation of the Episode, formed by imitations of the 3rd Counter-subject and farther on, by a fragment of the 2d combined with the 3d C.S.

Fragment
Imitation.
Imitation.
of the subject by diminution.
Fragments by contrary movement.
Imitation of
Id.
Fragment of the 3d C.S.
Id.

this fragment. Sub-
ject and the subject inverted, combined together.
Id

Counter-subject on the subj. inverted and diminished.
Fragment of the subject transposed into the relative Major but by contrary movement and by diminution.
Answer
Answer to
Reply to
to the Counter-subj.
the subject inverted and by diminution.

Counter-sub.
the subject diminished and inverted.
Reply of the Answer
Counter-subj.
Subject.
Episode compd of the 1st part of the subject inverted.

Fragment of the
Imitation
2d Counter-subject combined with a fragment of the 3d
Imitation.
Fragment of the 3d C.S.
of the fragment of the 2d Counter-subj.

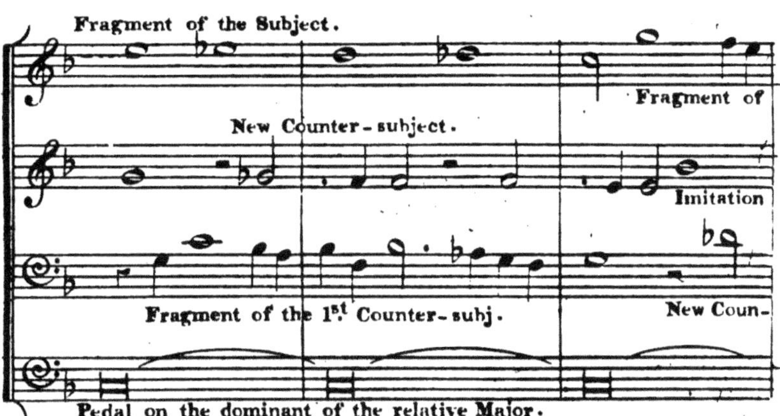
Fragment of the Subject.
Fragment of
New Counter-subject.
Imitation
Fragment of the 1st. Counter-subj.
New Coun-
Pedal on the dominant of the relative Major.

the 1st. Counter-subj.
of the fragment of the Subject.
ter-subject.

Fragment of the Counter-subject of the subject inverted.
Imitations of this fragment.
Fragment of the subj.
Idem.
Fragment of the 1st C. S.
Idem.
Subject by augmentation.

Stretto.
Subject.
Answer closer to the subject.
Subject.

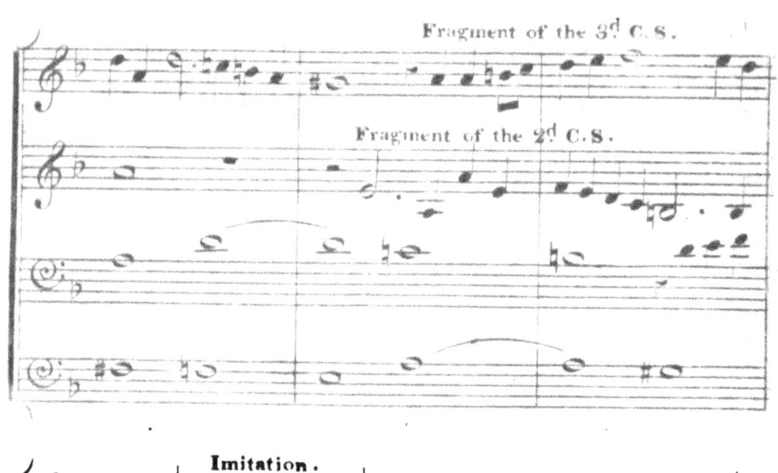
Fragment of the 3d C.S.
Fragment of the 2d C.S.

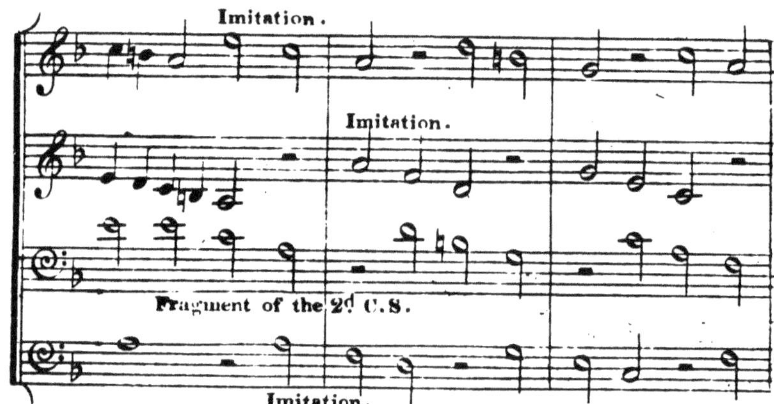
Imitation.
Imitation.
Fragment of the 2d C.S.
Imitation.

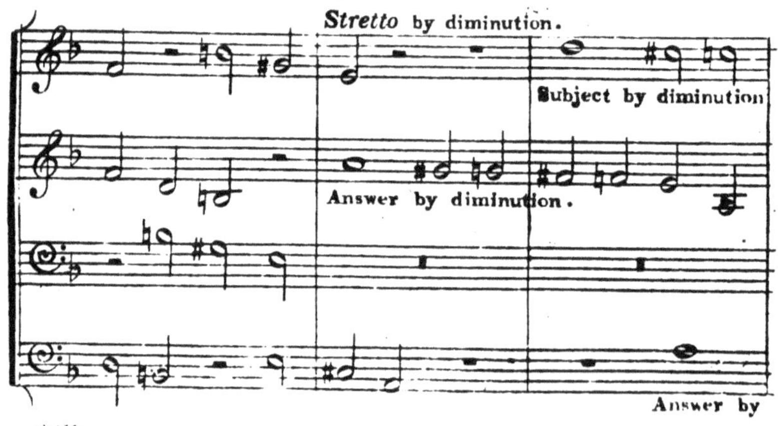
Stretto by diminution.
Subject by diminution
Answer by diminution.
Answer by

brought closer to the Answer.
Subject by diminution, brought closer.
diminution.
Subject by diminution.
Answer still closer.
Subject by diminution.
Answer.
Fragment of the 3d C.S.
Fragment of the 3d Counter-subj.

Answer in contray motion
and by diminution.
Answer proceeding with the subjects and
answers diminished and inverted.
Subject the same.
Answer in contrary motion and by diminution.
3d. Counter-subj.
Id.
Id.

Id.
Continuation of this Episode on a Pedal, supporting various artifices.
Stretto by diminution on the Pedal.
Subj. by diminution.
Answer.
Answer by diminution.
Subject.

Frag.t of the 3.d C.S.
Fragment of the 2.d C.S.

Imitation of the fragment of the 3d C.S.
Fragment of the
2d Counter-subj.
Imitation of the fragment of the 2d C.S.
Fragment of the 3d C.S.

Remark.

We have not hitherto spoken of the *Plagal* Cadence which is often met with in ancient compositions.

The Ancients termed *Authentic* that Cadence which we now call *Perfect*, that is to say the progression from the dominant to the Tonic.

They gave the name of *Plagal Cadence* to the progression from the *Sub-dominant* to the *Tonic*, and often concluded their Compositions by this sort of Cadence, always making the chord of the Tonic major, whatever mode the piece might be in. This Cadence was peculiar to the Plagal tones of the ecclesiastical modes.

TONAL FUGUE of great length, in 8 PARTS for TWO CHOIRS.

Imitation in the 10th.
Part which proposes another Counter-subject.
-li a - - - - - - - - - - - - men a - - - - - - - - - - - - - -
Answer.
Et vi - - - - tam ven-tu-ri
-men
Imitation in the unison of the 3d C.S.
Answer of the 2d C.S.
a - - - - - - - - - - - - men a - - - - - - - - - - -
Answer of the 1st C.S.
- - - men a - - - - - - - - - - - - - -

3d Counter-subj.
Part ad libitum.
men
a
Imitation in the 10th
sæ cu li a
men
Part which proposes a new C.S.
Part ad libitum.
a
men
a
Part ad libitum.
men
a
Imitation in the 8ve below the 3d subj.
men
a
men

Part ad libitum.
Answer to the other counter-subj. proposed.
a
men
a
Subject resumed.
Et
vi
1st Counter subj.
A
men
men
ad libitum.
2d C.S.
a
men
a

Answer to the new Counter-subj.
- - men
a
3d Counter subj.
men
Imitation in the 10th
tam ven-tu-ri
sæ
cu- -li a
Imitation in the unison.
men
a
ad libitum.
a
men

Answer to the 2d new Counter-subj.
men
a
Part ad libitum.
a
men
Answer of the 1st new C.S.
3d C.S.
men a
men a
Answer to the Subj.
Et vi tam ven-tu-ri sae cu
Answer to the 2d Counter-subj.
men a
Answer to the 1st Counter-subj.
a
men
men

Episode introducing the dominant on which the Subject is resumed.
-men
a -
Imitation in the unison.
a -
- - - men a - - - - men
a - - - - - - - -
Imitation in the 10th
- li a - men
- men.

- men
a
a
men
a

1st Counter-subj.
men a
men
2d and
men a
men
Return of the Subj.
Et vi

men
Answer to the Subj.
a
3d Counter-subject.
men
Answer to
a
Answer somewhat
Et vi
Answer to
tam ven-tu-ri sæ cu li a

a - - - - - - - - men
- men
1st C.S.
a - men a - - men a - - - - - -
the 2d Subject.
3d Counter-subj.
- men
closer to the Subj.
1st new C.S.
- tam ven - tu - ri sae - - - - - cu - - li a - - - -
Subject closer to the Answer.
Et vi - - -
the 1st new Counter-subj.
2d C.S.
- men a - -

Answer to the Subj. by
et
a-men a--men
a-
men
a
men
tam ven-tu-ri
sæ
cu
li
a
men
a

augmentation mixed with the Counter-subjects.

Episode which in

modulating brings in the Answer by augmentation in the relative Minor Key.

a - - - - - - - - men
a - - - - - - -
et
vi - - - - - -
a - - - - - - - - - men
a - -
. . . . . a - - men
a - - - - - - men
a - - - - - - - - - - - - - - - - - - -
- men
et
vi - - - - - -
a - - - - - - - - - - - - - - -

tam ven tu ri sæ cu
a
men a men a
tam ven tu ri sæ cu
men

Episode continues always modulating.
- men a - - - - - - - - - - - - - - - men a - -
- men
- - li a - - -
- men
Subj. in the sub-dominant.
- men a - - - - - - - men Et vi - - - -
- men a - - - - - - - men
- - li a - - - - - - men a - - - - - -
Et vi - - - - tam ven - tu - ri sae - - cu - li

a
men a
men
Subj. in A minor.
Et vi tam ven-tu-ri
tam ven-tu-ri sae-cu-li
a
a men a
men
a

-men a-men a-men a-men
-men a-men a-men a-men
a-men a-men a-men
sæ-cu-li a-men a-men
-men a
a

a
men
men
men a-men a-men
men a-men a-men

men
a
a
a

- men
a
a
a
- men
- men

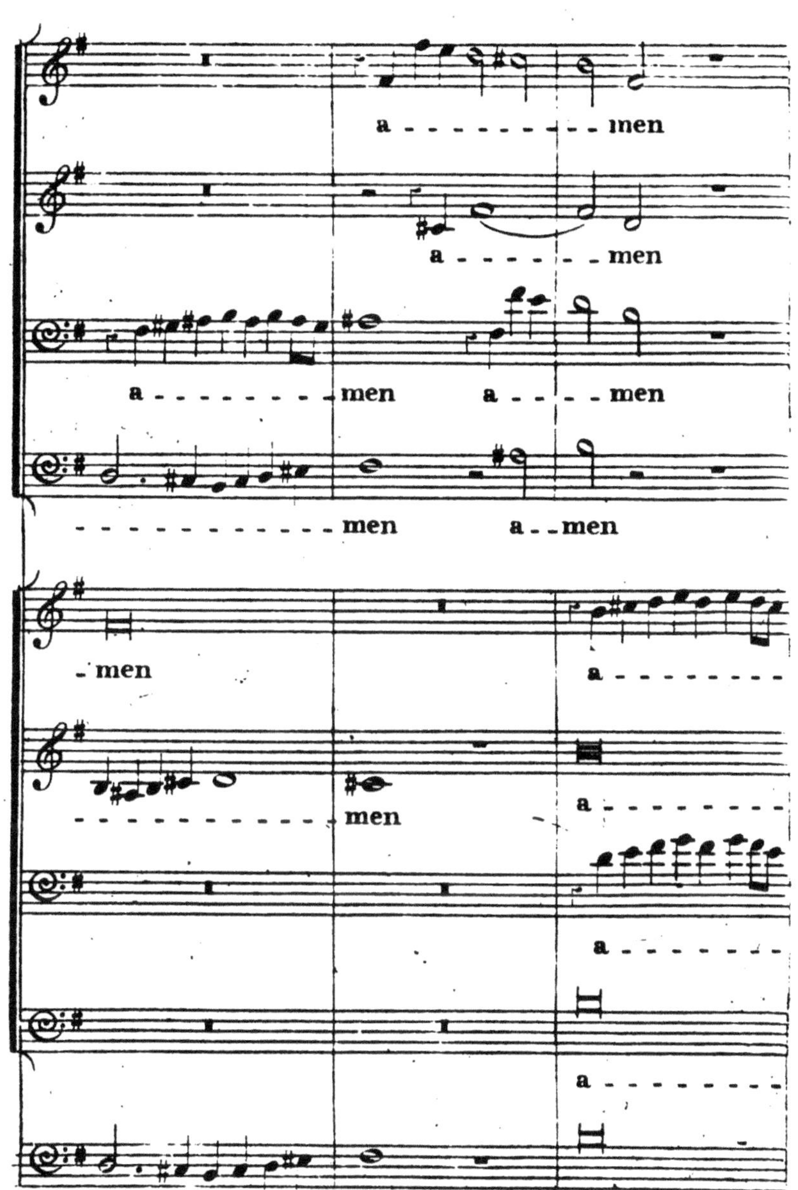
a - - - - - - - - - - men
a - - - - - - - men
a - - - - - - - - - men a - - - - men
- - - - - - - - - - - - - men a - - men
- men
a - - - - - - - -
- - - - - - - - - - - - - men
a - - - - - - - -
a - - - - - - - -
a - - - - - - - -

a - - - - - - - - - - - - men
a - - - - - - - -
a - - - - - - - - - - - - men
a - - - - - - - -
a - - - - - - - - - - - men
a - - - - - - - -
a - - - - - - - - - - - - men
a - - - - - - - -
- - - men
a - - - - - - - - men
- men
a - - - - - - - - - - men
- - - men
a - - men
- men
a - - - - - men

-men a--
---men a------men a------
-men a-------men a--
---men a------
a----------men a--men a--
a---------men a-men a-men a--
a----------men a-men a-men a--
a------------men a--men a--

-men a - - men a - - men
-men a - - men a - - men
-men a - - men a - - men
-men a - - men a - - men

men a men.
men.
men a men.
men.
a men.
Subject and Counter
a men. Et vi
a men. A
a men.

- subject inverted with alterations -
-tam ven-tu-ri sæ - - - - - -cu- -li a - - - - - - - -
- - - men a - - - - - - - - - - - men a - - - - - - - -

Answer the same.
Et vi - - - - tam ven - tu - ri sæ - - - - - - cu -
- men a - - - - - - - - - - men a - - - - - - - - - - - -
- - - - - - - - - - - - men a - - - - - - - - - - -

Et vi
A
li a
men a men
men a men

-tam ven-tu-ri sae - - - - - - cu-li a - - - - - - - -
- - - - men a - - - - - - - - - - men a - - - - - - - - -
- men a - - - - - - - - - - - - - - - - men a - - - -
a -
a - - - - - - - - men a - - - - - - - -

Et vi - - - tam ven - tu - ri sæ - - - - - - cu -
men a - - - - - - - - - men a - - - - - - - - - - -
- - - - - - - - - - - - men a - - - men a -
- men a - - - - - - - - - - - - - - -
- men a - - - - - - - - - - - - - - - - - -
- - - - - - - - - - - - - - men a - - men a -

- li a - men a - - - - -
- - - - - - men a - - - - - - - - - men a - - -
- men a - men
- men
- - - - - - - - - - - - - - - men a - - -
- men . . . . a - men . . . . a - -
Et vi - - - -

- - - men a - - - - - - - - men a - - - - - - - - - - - - -
- - - - - - - - - - - - - - - - - men a - - - - - -
a - - - - - - men a - men
Et vi - - - - tam ven - tu - ri
a - - - - - - men a - - - - - -
- - - - - - - - - - - - men a - - - - - - - - - men a -
- - - - - - - - - - men a - - - - - - - - - - - - - - - - - -
- tam ven - tu - ri sæ - cu - li a - men a - - -

men a - men a - men
- men a - - men a -
a - - men a -
sæ - cu - li a - men a - men
- men a -
- men a -
- men a - men
- men a - men a - men a -

a - - - men a -
- - - - - - - - men a - - - - - - - - - - - - - - - - -
- - - men a - - - - - - - - - - - - - - - - -
a - - - - - men a - - - - - - - - - - - - - - men
- - men a -
- - - men a - - - men a - - - men a - - - men
a - - - - - - men a - - men a - -
- - - men a - - - men a - - - - - - -

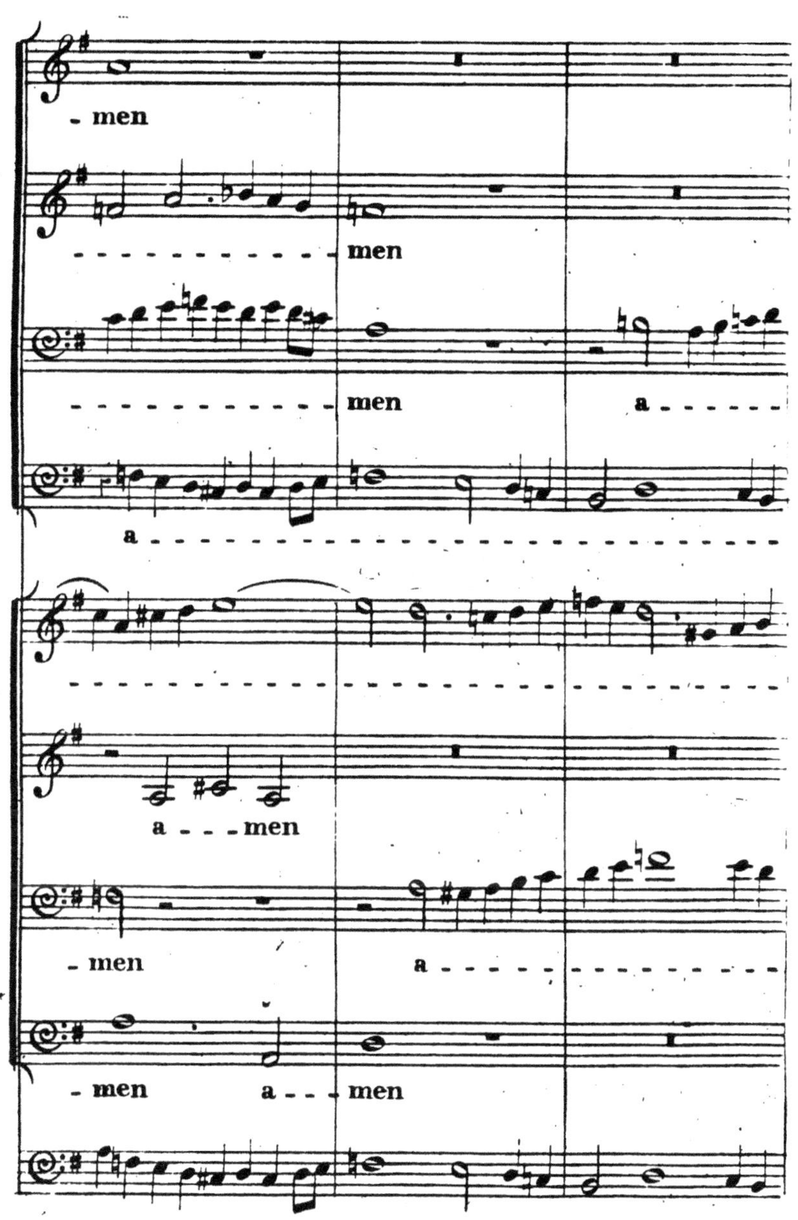
- men
- - - - - - - - - - - - - men
- - - - - - - - - - - - - men
a - - - - - -
a -
a - - - men
- men
a - - - - - - - - - - - - - - -
- men
a - - - men

Subject in A minor, and in its primitive form.

Episode which

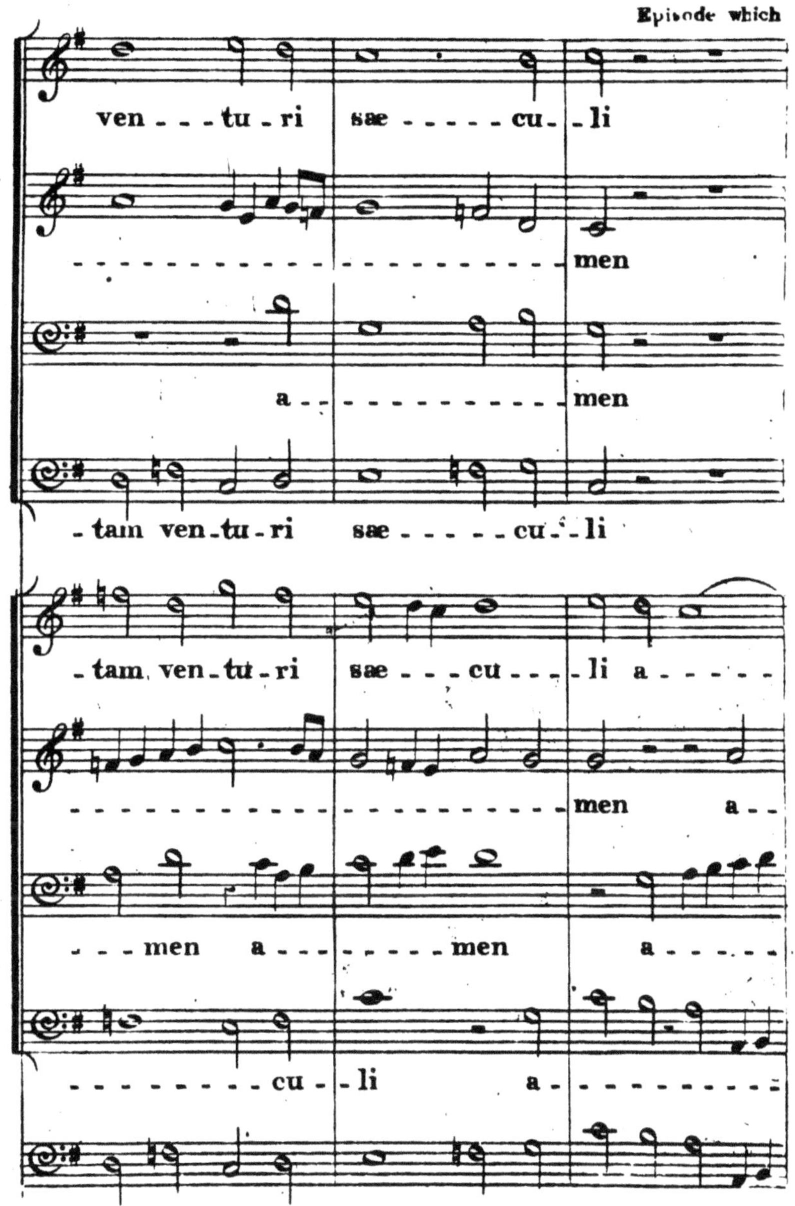

modulates and the two choirs
imitate each other alternately.
a
a
men
a
men
a
men
men
men
men a
a
men
a

men
a
men
a
men
a
men
a
men
a
men
a
men
a
men
a
a

a - men
a , - men
a - - - - - - - - - - - - - men
a - - - - - - - - men
- men
a - - - - - - - - - -
- men
a - - - - - - - - - -
- men
a - - - - - - - - - -
- men
a - - - - - - - - - -

a ---------- men
a ---------- men
a ---------- men
a ---------- men
------------ men et .... vi ----
--- men a ------------
--- men a ----------------
--- men et ...... vi ---------

et .... vi - - - tam
a - - - - - - - - - - - - - - - - - men
a - - - - - - - - - - - - - - - - - men
et - vi - - - - - - - - - - - - - - tam
- tam
et
- - - - - - men
a - -
- men
a - - - - - -
- men
et ....

a - - - - - - - - - - men
a - - - - - - - - - - - - - - men a - -
a - - - - - - - - - - - - - - men
ven - tu - - ri sæcu - li
. . . . . vi - - - - tam a - - - - - - - - -
- - - - - - - - - - - - - - - - - men a - - - - - - -
- - - - - - - - - - - - - men a - - - - - - - - - - - - - -
vi - - - - - - - - - tam ven - tu - - ri

a - - - - - - - - men a - - - - - - - - - - - men a - - -
- men a - - - men
a - - - - - - - - - men a - - - - - - - - - - - men
a - - - - - - - - - men a - - - - - - - - - - - men
- men a - - - - - - - men a - - - - - - - - - - - men
- - - men a - - - men a - - - - men
- men a - - - - - - - - - men a - - - - - -
sæculi a - - - - - - - - - - men a - -

men a
a men a men a men
a men a
a men a
a men a
a men a men a men
men a men
men a men

- - - men a - - - - men a - - - - - - - - - - - - - -
. . . . a - men a - - - - - - - - - - - - - - - - - -
- - - - - - - - - men a - - - - - - - - - - - - - - - -
- - - - - - - - - - - - - men
- - - - - - - - - - - - - men a - - - - - -
a - - - - - - - - - men
a - - - - - - - - - - - - - men
a - - - - - - - - - - - - - - - - - men a - - - -

-men a - - - - - - - men a - - - - - -
- - - - - - men a - - - - - - - - - - - - - - men
-men a - - - - - - - - - - - - - - - - men a - - - - - - - -
et vi - - - - - tam ven-tu-ri sæ-cu- -li
- - - - - - - - - - - - - - - - - - - men a - -
et vi - - -
a - - - - - - - - - - - - - - - - -
- - - - - men a - - - - - - - - - -

men
men
a
a men a
men a men a
tam ven tu ri sæ cu li. a
men
men a

a
men
a
a
men
a
men
a
men
a
men
men
a
men
a
men
a
a
men
a
men
a

men a
men a men a
men a men a
men a men
men a
men a
men a

men.
men a men.
men a men.
a men.
men a men.
men a men.
men a men.
men a men a men.

Stretto.
Et vi - - - tam ven - tu - ri sae - - - - - cu - -
Et vi - - - -
A - - - - - - - - - - - - - - - - - - - men a - -
A - - - - - - - - - - - - - - men a - - - - - - - -

-li a - - - - - - men a - - - - - - - - - - - - - - - -
-tam ven-tu-ri sæ - - - cu - - - - li a - - - - - - -
- - - - - - - - - - - - men
a - - - - - - - - - - -
a - - - - - - - - - - - - - - -
- - - - - - - - - - - - - men a - - - - - - - - - - - - - -
Et vi - - - - tam ven-tu-ri

-men
-men
-men a - - - - - - - - - - - - - - - - - - men
-men a - - men . . . . a - - - - - - - -men a - - - - - -
-men . . . . a - - - men a - - - - - - - -
sæ - - - - - - cu - - li a - - - - - - - men
Et vi - - - tam ven-tu-ri sæ - - - - - - cu - -

Stretto with the 3 Counter-subjects.
a
a
a
-men.
-men.
-li.

men
men
men
a
a
Idem.
a

a
a
a
men
men
men
men
a

Symmetrical progression by the Subject in augmentation.

a - - - men a - - men a - men
- - - men a - - men a - men
- men a - - men a - - men a - men a - - - - - - - -
sæ - cu - - li a - - men a - men a - - - - - - - - men
- ri . . . . . sæ - cu - - li a - men a - -
a - - - men a - - men a - men a - - - -
- - - men a - - men a - men a - -
- - - - - - - men a - - men a - men a - men a - -

a - - - - - - men a - - - - - - men a - - - - - - - -
a - - - - - - - men a - - - - - - - men a - - - - - -
- men a - - - - - - - men a - - - - - men a - -
a - - - - - - - men a - - - - - - men a - men
- - - - - - - - - - men a - - - - men a - men
- - - - - - - men a - - men a - men
- - - - men a - men
- men

men
men
men
men
et vi tam ven tu ri
Stretto still closer.
et vi tam ven tu ri sæ
a

Idem.

et vi - - - tam ven - - tu - ri sæ - - -
et vi - - - tam ven - tu - - ri sæ - - - - - cu -
a - - - - - - - - - - - - - - - - - - - men
sæ - - cu - li a -
- - - cu - - li a -
- men
et

-cu--li a------------------men
-li a-----------------men
et vi---
a-------------------men et
-men a---------------men
---men
vi---tam ven--tu-ri sæ------cu-li a-
et vi----tam ven-tu-ri sæ---cu-li

a - men
a - - - - - - - - - - - - - - - - - - - men et
-tam ven-tu--ri sæ - - - - - - cu-li a - - - - men
vi- - -tam ven--tu-ri sæ-cu-li a- - -men
et
et
- men et vi-
a - - - - - - - - - - - - - - - - - - men a - - -

et .... vi - - - - tam vi - tam ven
..... vi - - - - tam ven - - - tu - - - - ri ven
a - - - - - - men a - - - - - - men et vi - tam
a - - - men a - - - men vi
..... vi - - - tam ven - - - tu - ri sæ
..... vi - - - tam ven - - - tu - - - - ri
- - - tam ven - - - tu - - - - ri sæ - - - cu
- men a - - - men a - - - - - - - men et

tu - - - - ri sae - - - cu - li sae - - - - - - cu -
tu - - - - ri sae - - - - - - - - - - - - - - - cu - - -
ven - tu - ri ven - tu - ri sae - - - cu -
- tam ven - tu - - - - ri sæ - - - - - - - - - - - - - cu - - -
- - - - - - - - - - - - - - - - - cu - - - - - - - - - li . . . . .
sae - cu - - - - - - - -
- li et vi - - - tam ven - tu - - - - ri sae - cu - - -
vi - - - tam ven - tu - - - - - - - ri sae - - - - - cu -

- li a - men a - - -
- li a - - - - - - - - - - men
- li
- li a - - - - - - - - - men
..... a - - - men ....
- li a - - - - - - - -
- li a - - - - - - - men
- li a - - - men a - - men

men .... a
a men a
a
a men a men a
men a men
a men
a men

- men
- men a - men
- men
- - - - - - - - - men a - - - - men a - - men a - - -
a -
a -
a - - - men a - - men a - - -
a -

Pedal on which the closest Stretto of the Subject is introduced as well as the Counter-subjects.

- - - - cu - - li a - - - - - - - men a - - - - - - men
- - - - cu - - li a - men
- - li a - - - - - - - men a - men a - - men a - men
- - tu - - - - ri sæ - - - - - - cu - li a - - - - men a - -
sæ - - cu - li a - - - - men a - - - - - - - - - - - - - -
sæ - cu - - li a - men a - - men a - - - - - -

a
men
a
a
men
a
men
a
men
men

Final Episode
men . . . a-men a - - - men a - - -
a - - - - - - - - - - men a - men a - - - men
men a - - - men a - - -
a - - men a - men a - - - men
men a - men a - - - men
a - men a - - - men a - men a - - - men a - - -
men a - - - - - men a - - - men a - - -
a - - men a - men a - - - men

introducing the conclusion of the Fugue.

a - - - - - - - - men
- men . . . . . a - - - - - - - - - - - - - - - - men a -
- - - - - - men a - - - - - - - - men a - - - - - - - - - - - - -
- - - - - - men . . . . a - - - - - - - - - - - -
a - - - - - men
- men . . . . . a - - - men a - - - - - - -
- - - - - - men a - - - - - - - - men a - - - - - - -
a - - - - - - - - - men a - - - - - -

a
men
a
a
men a
men
a
men
a

Plagal cadence
to finish.
-men amen a-men amen a-men a--men.
-men amen a-men amen a-men a--men.
-men amen a-men amen a-men a--men.
-men amen a-men amen a-men a--men.
-men amen a-men amen a-men a--men.
-men amen a-men amen a-men a--men.
-men amen a-men amen a-men a--men.
-men amen a-men amen a-men a--men.

STRICT FUGUE.

for 2 CHOIRS, by JOSEPH SARTI.

pa
1st Counter-subject.
a
Tasto Solo.

2d Counter-subj.
- - - - tris in glo-ria De - - - - i patris a -
Answer to Subj.
Cum sancto spi-ri-tu in gloria De-i pa - - - - - -
Answer of
a - -

men a men a
tris
Part ad lib:
men a
the Counter-subj.

Part ad libitum.
men a
Part ad libitum.
Answer to the 2d C.S.
a men in glo-ria
Subject.
Cum sanc-to spi-ri-tu in
men a

men
De - - - - - i patris a - - - men a - -
glo - ria De - i pa - - - - - - - - - - - - - - - -
Ist Counter-subj.
a - - - - - - - - - - - - - -

Answer to the Subject.
Cum sancto spi_ritu in gloria De_i
in glo_ria De i patris a
_ _ men a
_tris in glo_ria De _ _ _ _ i.
_ men a
Part ad libitum imitating a portion of the
_ men a

pa -tris
- -men
- - - - - - - - - - - - - - -men in glo-ria De-i pa- - -
patris a- -men a- -men a- - - - - - - - -
Answer to 1st C.S.
a -men
- - - - - - - - - - - -men a- - - - -men a- -men
melody proposed by the Counter-tenor.
- - - - - - - - - - - - - - - -men a- -men a- - - -
- -men ..... a -

Portion of the 1st Counter-subj.
a - men
Subject.
Cum sancto spi - - ri - - tu in glo - ria
Imitation of the
- - - - - - - - - tris
a - - - - - - -
- - - - - - - - - men
a - - - -
Portion of a close imitation of the Answer.
Cum sanc - - to
Answer curtailed.
- - - - - - - men
Cum
sancto spi - - ri -
- - - - - - - men
Cum sanc - to

Idem.
a
De - i pa
above portion of the Counter - subj.
men
men
Part ad libitum imitating a portion of the Subject.
spi - - - - - ri - - - tu in glo - - - - - ri - a
Answer of the Subj.
Cum sancto spi - - ri - tu in
- tu in glo - - ri - - a De - - i pa - tris a - -
spi - ri - tu in glo - ria De - - i pa - - - tris

men
tris a men a
a men a men a
Ist Counter-subj.
a
De i pa tris a
glo-ria De-i pa
men a
a men

Episode formed by an imitation of the Counter-subj. modulating in

order to return to the principal Key on which the Answer to the Subject re-appears in the dominant.

Portion of the 2d C.S.
in glo_ri_a
Portion of the 1st C.S.
a
Part ad libitum.
De_i pa - - - - - tris a - - - -
a - - - - - - men
Answer in the Octave of the dominant more complete.
Cum sanc_to spi_-ri_tu in
- - - - men
but curtailed.
spi_-ri_tu in glo_ria De_-i pa - - - tris
Portion of the 2d C.S.
in glo_ri_a De - - - - - i patris a - -

De - - - i patris
- - - - - - - - - - - - - - - - men
- - - - - - - - - - - - - men
a - - - - - men
glo-ria De-i pa - - - - - - - - - - - - - - - - - - -
Imitation of the 1st Subj.
a - - men
a - - - - -
1st Counter-subject.
a - - - - - - - - - - - - - - - - -
- - - - men

Parts ad lib:
a - men a - men
a - men a - men
a - men a - men
a - men a - men
Episode similar to the preceding which after modulating stops on the dominant.
- tris a
- men a - men
Part ad lib:
a - men a - men a

Episode in which is introduced the
Answer to the Subject and the
Cum sancto spiri_tu in
Cum sancto spi_ri_ _tu
Cum sancto spi_ri_tu in glori_a
Cum sancto spi_ri_tu in
- - - - - - - - - - - - - men
- - - - - - - - - - - - men
Cum
Cum
- - - - - - - - - - - - - men

repercussion of the latter
closer to the Answer.
glo-ria De-i pa-tris De-i pa
in glo-ri-a
De-i pa-tris
glo-ri-a De-i pa-tris De-i pa
Episode answering the other by an imitation in the unison.
Cum sancto spi-ri-tu in gloria De-i pa-
sanc-to spi-ri-tu in glo-ri-a
sanc-to spi-ri-tu in glo-ri-a
Cum sanc-to spi-ri-tu in glo-ria De-i

tris a
a
a men
tris De i patris De i
tris in glo ria De
De i pa tris
a
De i pa tris a men a
patris De i patris De i patris a

men
a
men
a
Cum sancto spi_ritu in glo_ria De_i
patris a_ men a_ men a_ men a_
_i De_i patris a_men a_men
men a_men a_men
men a_men a_men
_men De_i patris a_men a_men

Imitation in contrary motion.
-men
a
-men in glo
pa - - - tris
a
-men a - men a
The episode goes on introducing a portion of the Counter-subj. in contrary motion.
a
a
in glo - - ri - - a
a - men a - men

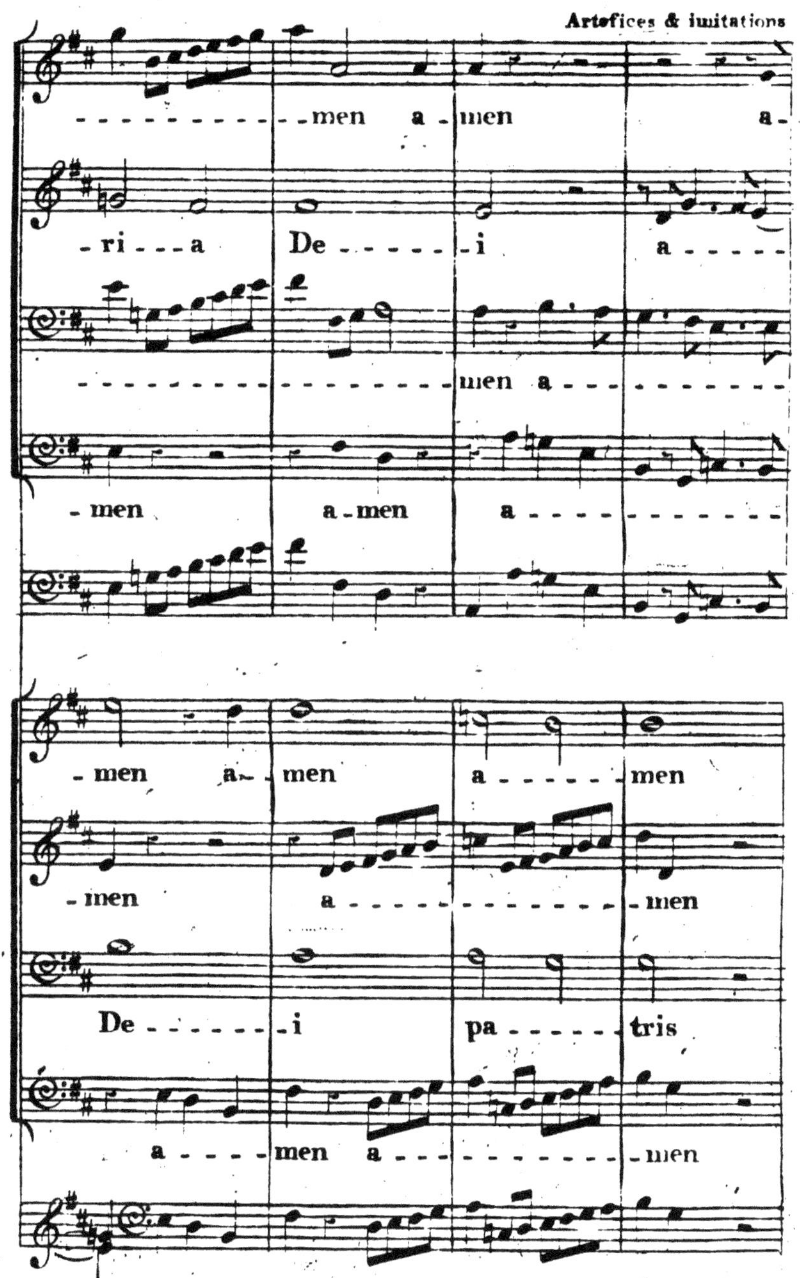
men a - men a -
ri - a De - i a
men a
men a - men a
men a - men a - men
men a - men
De - i pa - tris
a - men a - men

by augmentation of the first Counter-subj. modulating to the sub-dominant and then returning to the principal Key.

The Episode continues

by a portion of the 1st Counte-subj. imitated and drawn closer; after modulating this episode closes in F♯ minor.

men a
men
a
men
men
men
a
men
men a
men
men a
men
men
a
men
men
a
men

Stretto.
Cum sancto
Cum sancto spi_ri_tu in
Cum
Cum
Portion of the 1st Counter-subj.
a
a

spi-ri-tu in glo-ria De-i pa----tris a------
glo-ria De-i patris cum sancto spi-ri-tu in gloria
sancto spi-ri-tu in glo-ria De----i pa------
sancto spi-ri-tu in glo-ria De-i patris a------
Imitation of this inversion.
-men Cum sancto spi-ri-tu in glo-ria
-----------men Cum sancto spi-ri-tu in
a------------------------men
Subject nearly inverted.
Cum sancto spi-ri-tu in gloria De-i

De-i pa - - tris a - - - - - - - men a - - - -
- - - - - - - - - - - - tris a - - - - - - - - - - - - - -
Pedal.
De-i pa - - - - - - tris a - - - - - - - -
glo-ria De-i pa - - tris a - - - - - - - - -
a - - - - - - - - - men a - - - - - - - - -
Pedal.
pa - - tris a - - - - - - - - - - - - - - - -

men
men
men
men
men
men
men
men
men

Conclusion.
a - men a - men
a - men a - men
a - men a - men
a - men a - men
a - men a - - men
a - men a - - men
a - men a - - men
a - men a - - men

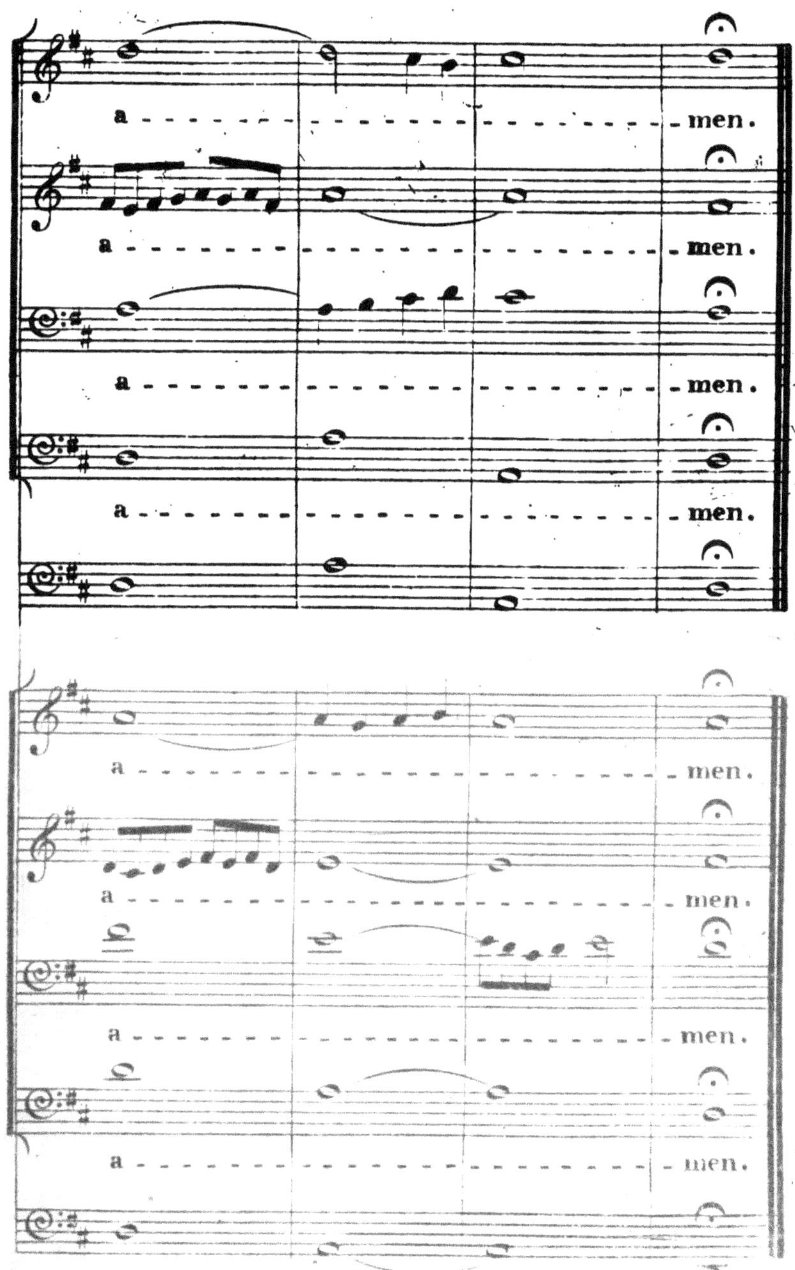
a - - - - men.
a - - - - men.
a - - - - men.
a - - - - men.
a - - - - men.
a - - - - men.
a - - - - men.
a - - - - men.

APPENDIX.

CANTI FIRMI, or SUBJECTS.

to serve for LESSONS *in Strict Counterpoint.*

In C.

8.
9.
10.
11.
12.

13.
14.
Variation instead of the three last bars.
15.
In D.
16.
17.
18.

19.
20.
21.

22.
In E.
23.
24.
25.
26.

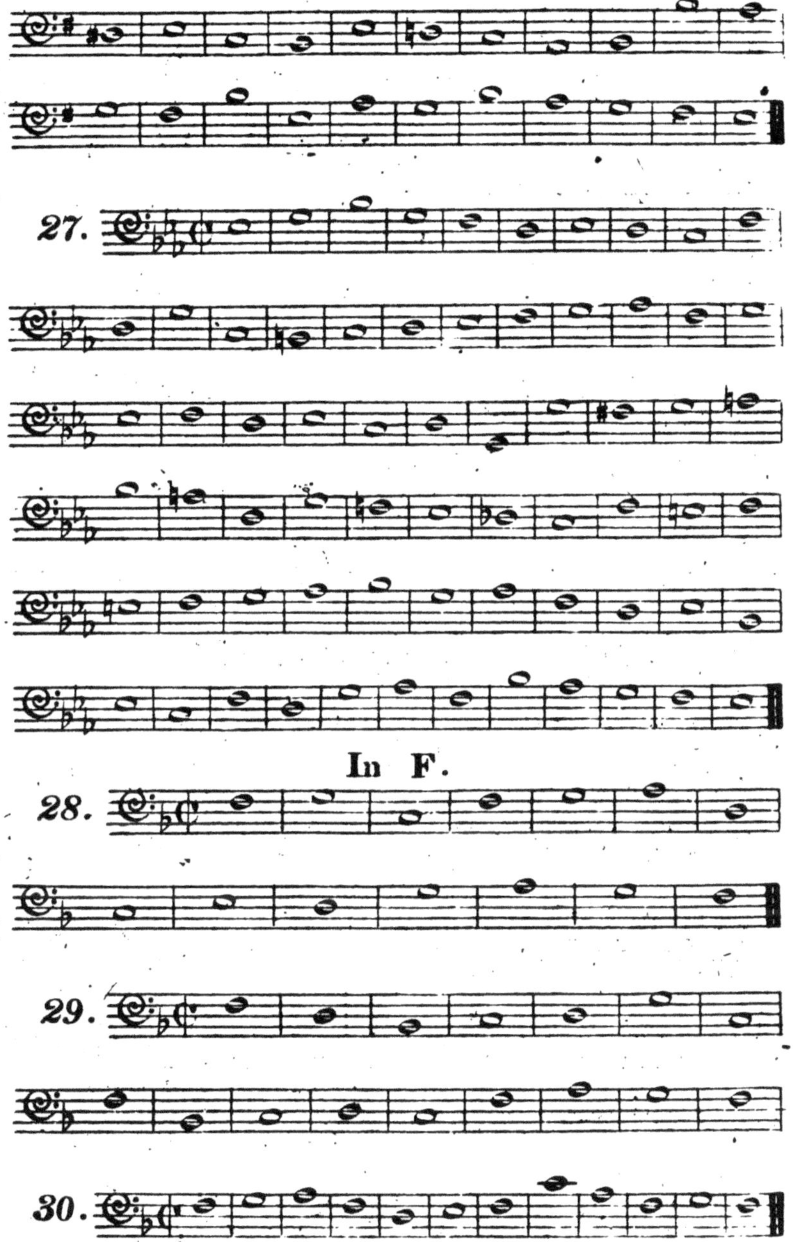
27.
In F.
28.
29.
30.

31.
32.
33.
In G.
34.
35.

36.
37.
38.
39.
40.

41.

In A.

42.

43.

44.

45.

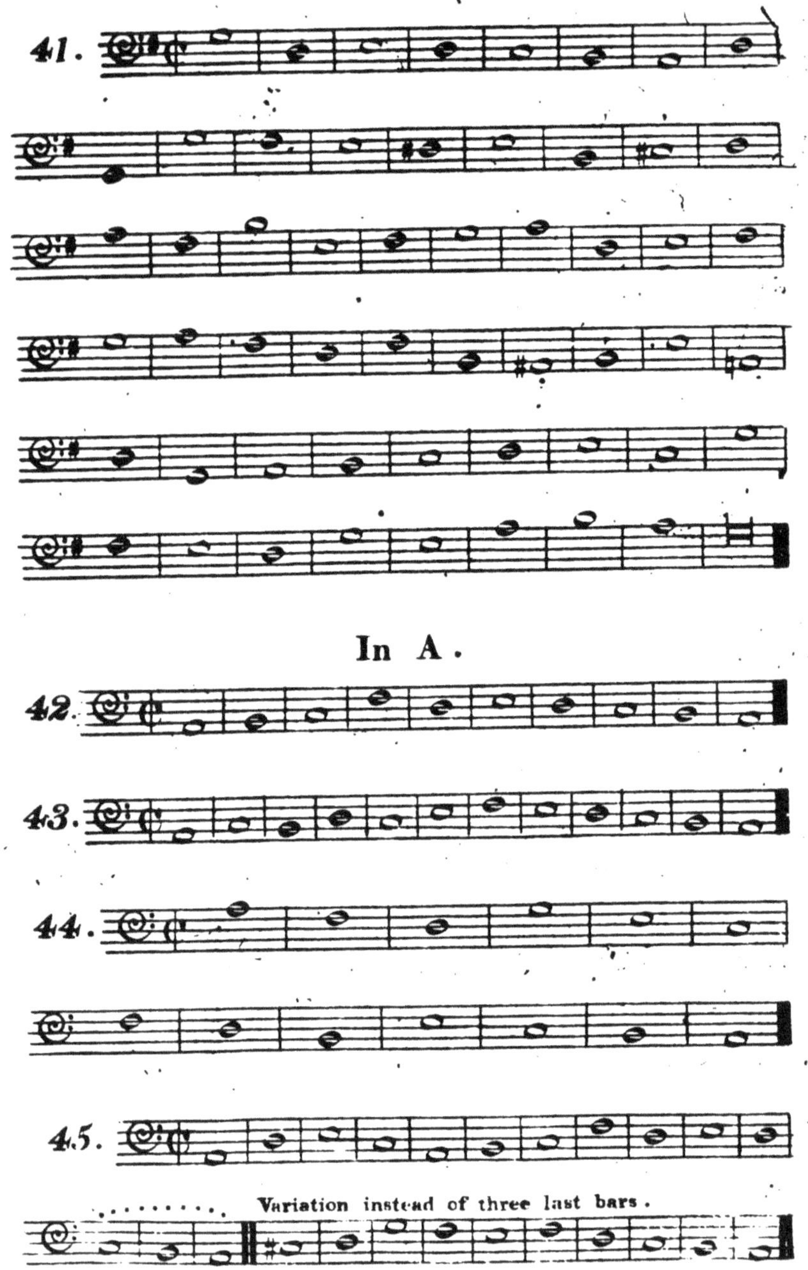

46.
47.
48.
49.

In B.

BASSES for Counterpoint in 8 Parts, and for TWO CHOIRS.

3.
4.

5.
6.

7.
8.

9.
10.

11.

12.

www.ingramcontent.com/pod-product-compliance
Lightning Source LLC
LaVergne TN
LVHW081352060426
835510LV00013B/1791
9781628451733